HOW TO BECOME RICH FROM THE CORONAVIRUS WAR

More than one strategy for profit without capital

AHMED AWAD

1st Edition Copyright © 2020 AHMED AWAD
All rights reserved.
ISBN: 978-1-716-83023-5

CONTENT

* INTRODUCTION.
* HOW TO CREATE WEALTH.
* WHAT IS THE WAY FOR A FIRST MILLION DOLLARS.
* WHAT SHOULD I DO.
* THE FIELD OF DIGITAL MARKETING.
* THE FIELD OF PROFIT FROM ADVERTISING THROUGH CONTENT INDUSTRY.
* THE FIELD OF SELF-EMPLOYMENT.
* THE FIELD OF MICRO SERVICES.
* THE FIELD OF ELECTRONIC COMMERCE.
* THE FIELD OF TRADE IN THE STOCK MARKET.
* THE FIELD OF TRADE IN THE STOCK MARKET.
* THE FIELD OF DIGITAL CURRENCIES.
* CHAPTER 1 "DIGITAL MARKETING".
* CHAPTER 2 "CONTENT INDUSTRY".
* CHAPTER 3 "WEBSITES".
* CHAPTER 4 "E-COMMERCE".
* CHAPTER 5 "FACEBOOK MARKETPLACE".
* CHAPTER 6 "DIGITAL CURRENCIES"
* WARNINGS.

◆ ◆ ◆

Introduction

According to the report published by the Income Control Authority, titled, "Private Wealth," there were an estimated $ 15 trillion in wealth accumulated in the United States in the early 1990s, according to a more recent study by the Foundation, "Merrill Lindsey," In the United States, the amount of private wealth has increased to $ 27 trillion, but 90% of wealth is owned by only 10% of people. So the question must be: What do these 10% know and the remaining 90% are ignorant of? The answer is that the 10 percent rich know that the fastest way to get rich is by owning their own business, and they also know how to create income generating sources.

How to create wealth

First, read this brief study: While the world is witnessing the emerging crisis of the Coronavirus, which has negatively affected the global economy, a recent American study showed that the wealth of billionaires in the United States rose dramatically against the background of the spread of the new Corona virus epidemic in the world.

The study said that some of the richest people in the United States increased their wealth from March 18 to May 19 by 434 billion dollars, It also indicated that the number of billionaires increased in May from 614 to 630 billionaires, according to the news site "Russia Today". The study revealed the biggest beneficiaries of the pandemic, and said that Amazon CEO Jeff Bezos increased his wealth by $ 34.6 billion, while Facebook founder Mark Zuckerberg increased his wealth by 25.3 billion$.

What is the way for a first million dollars

Under the Coronavirus, a large number of people entered or will enter poverty due to unemployment and layoffs to reduce their numbers. There are many jobs that are threatened, you must take a serious step from now, and as the study showed, whoever has increased his income and achieved superstitious profits in light of the crisis prevailed The world has affected the global economy, but the excluded group from this are the owners of e-business activities and I will explain to you in detail about every activity that will earn you income, and if you working seriously it is very easy you become a millionaire in less than one year.

what should I do?

You want to work online and earn money from it, you searched a lot on the various sites and endless YouTube videos, but you do not find a satisfactory answer often. You may ask yourself what are the areas of profit from the Internet, and how do I choose the field that best suits my skills or experience in order to make the most of the terrible technology world.

In this book in particular I will give you a comprehensive overview from above about the main areas of profit from the Internet.

Imagine yourself now flying over the world of the Internet like a falcon, looking to see the full picture so that you can choose the appropriate field from the various domains of profit from the Internet, and swoop on it with full force and enthusiasm, just as the falcon crushes its prey, Profits from the Internet are very diverse, some of which require a lot of effort and experience, some of which require a lot of time, and some require some capital in order to start, Of course, in every field, there are many sub-fields, and there is a lot of details and information about the actual start in each field.

In this book I will give outline beginners to explain the idea of each field and then show you all the details to be choose and apply easily.

The field of digital marketing

Digital marketing is the primary focus and the first element in all areas of profit from the Internet. In fact, there is no field of profit from the Internet that does not need marketing, and when we say marketing here, we mean marketing through the Internet or digital or electronic marketing.

Although online marketing is a common and essential element in all areas of profit from the internet, it can be seen as a separate field and profits can be generated through it in many ways and strategies, In fact, every day you market something without knowing it. Remember, you're trying to convince a friend that a certain product is better than another? Or you try to persuade your father to use a specific service that may save him effort and money. In short, this is what marketing generally means, convincing a certain person that this product is good for them.

Certainly, you see a lot of advertisements, whether you are walking in the street, and you may find someone distributing promotional papers to you as well, and also on TV, these ads are intended to buy a specific service or product, The only thing is that you will do so as well, but only via the Internet, promoting a specific product or service in exchange for a fee. This return you get directly from the owner of the product or service, or you get from the difference between the sale and purchase price in the event that the product belongs to you?

Marketing is to put the product in front of the person who wants it at the right time. You can promote offers and products through websites, or through social media such as Facebook or YouTube completely free of charge, There are different types of e-marketing, such as commission marketing (in the corresponding type that you get is based on the results and sales you achieve), and direct marketing (in this type you get the return for promotion only regardless of the results).

Digital Marketing field characteristics:

*It requires patience and durability to make a profit.

* You can start for free without any capital.

* Programs, companies and service owners that you can promote are widely available.

* It is an interesting field, especially if you market something you love personally.

*It contains many branches, disciplines, methods and strategies.

The field of profit from advertising through content industry

Have you downloaded a program or movie from a site like (myegy or Arablionz) before? Didn't you notice that when you click on a specific link you are directed to a page with an ad, you wait for 5 seconds and then go to the download or watch page?

This page that you are viewing now you did not see at the beginning images and has this tag "AD" which means an advertisement, when you browse YouTube you will not find some ads displayed before or even while you are watching some videos, and you will also find ads in the search results as well.

In this field you mainly provide the place where the ads are shown, and of course this place must be attractive to the visitors (that is, they have something they want), in order for the ads to get views or clicks, You can create a website or YouTube channel, and profit from ads through various advertising programs such as AdSense.

Profit properties by advertising:

•It takes valuable industry and content to generate traffic or views for your content.

•It takes patience because you will not make a profit overnight.

•This method is characterized by the fact that every piece of content you manufacture can bring you a profit for several years.

•When you own a YouTube site or channel, you can combine profit from advertising, and you can also rely on commission marketing to others.

•This field needs to be tried and tested in order to find the best way for you to create good content.

The field of self-employment

Self-employment is to be the manager of yourself and your employer, this field is very common in the labor market on the ground and also on the Internet. You are offering your services and skills to those who need them for money.

You can be a designer, writer, programmer, montage

expert, fitness trainer and many other skills. These skills are needed by many people, especially on the Internet, and they will pay you money for your help, This field requires skill and experience, but who among us does not have any skill or experience, you can take advantage of your field of study, or your life experiences, or even learn a new skill you are as passionate about as graphic design. Even if you spend your day following up on social media sites, you can still profit from the field of self-employment, **Entrepreneurial field characteristics:**

•Your skill and expertise should stand out to potential clients, and this requires a lot of effort and focus.

•You can start in this area for free without capital.

•Self-employment can help you achieve a great income without taking on big responsibilities, and this is what distinguishes it from others.

•You can find customers to collaborate with them very easily through social media, as well as self-employment platforms.

•This field requires negotiation skill, to know how to offer your services to clients, and to get the best possible compensation for your time in order to avoid any problems.

The field of micro services

This field is also part of the field of self-employment, but it differs from it in several important points, This field is about sharing your time doing simple things for companies or entrepreneurs. For example, you can test some applications and express your opinion about them, or some programs or electronic services, There are companies that want to test their products and services before offering them to users, and they will pay you for that, and you can also work as an assistant for a business leader (virtual assistant), you can respond to emails or comments on social media pages, You can also provide simple services such as converting some videos to written text, or entering some data in Excel tables, for example.

What makes this field different from self-employment is that you do not need any specific skill or experience. All you have to do is just donate your time.

Micro services field properties:

•This field does not require experience as I mentioned, but the material return from it is much lower.

•This field is more suitable for those who already have jobs or another source of income and want an additional source.

The field of electronic commerce

This field is very suitable if you like to make things in your hand or like to trade in general. You can sell anything these days anywhere in the world. Perhaps you are skilled in handicrafts and distinctive decorations, or you know the sources of buying any product in bulk.

You can sell your product by building an online store,

or you can sell on different sales platforms such as Facebook and Etsy, and it has become very easy.

Ecommerce properties:

•You must have capital to start in this area.

•You must have some basic marketing skills to properly promote your product.

•You must provide after-sales service and build a good relationship with your customers in order to ensure that they buy from you continuously.

•This field has excellent profits and you can invest part of your profits in your project so that your business grows more and more.

•This field will enable you to build very good relationships, which will greatly benefit in your life.

•This field needs to be creative and different from others, in order for people to buy from you and not from others.

The field of trade in the stock market

Perhaps you have prior knowledge of the stock market and the field of stock trading, this field is also a trade, but in a different way, you buy company stocks at a certain price, and then sell them at a higher price.

This field is considered the best in terms of profit, for this you will find that most of the wealthy people in the world have collected a large part of their wealth from this field, and today, due to the terrible development in the world of information technology, you can trade in the stock market shares in any market in the world from your home very easily.

This money is divided into two types:

Trading in corporate stocks (which is the most common method) Currency trading or as it is called Forex, The second type is trade as well, and in order for different currencies such as the dollar, the euro and the pound, as you know there is a difference between the purchase and sale price for each currency, and the prices of these customers are constantly changing due to supply and demand.

This is very similar to trading in corporate stocks, whose prices change as well due to market changes in supply and demand, but the currency trading market is separate in itself.

Characteristics of the field of trade in the stock market:

•Working in this field requires experience reading the market and analyzing news in order to know when to buy and when to sell.

•This requires you to learn how to properly use trading platforms, and this takes some time.

•You must have a significant amount of capital to start and make profits in this field.

•Profit money is not fixed in this field, you may win after a day or after several years, so you must invest in more than one share or currency.

•This field is volatile and full of adventures, there are those who became rich in several days, and there are those who lost all their money in moments.

The field of digital currencies

Have you ever heard of (blockchain technology) or have you heard of digital currencies like (Bitcoin)? And if you haven't heard about this before, let me just explain it to you.

You know what banknotes we trade every day - like the pound, dinar, and riyal - are gold securities, which people used to use in trading in the past, such as buying and selling, When the need arose to keep these funds in designated places (such as banks), people began using financial bonds (bank notes proving their ownership of gold) to buy and sell, and from this the paper currencies appeared, In this modern era, information is gold, and because the information is very sensitive and important, and it must be secured on the Internet, this is why technology such as blockchain appeared, which helps in the process of circulating information and data completely safely and very complicated.

As a result of this, digital currencies emerged as a result of the process of exchanging information through this technology, and then after that, the process of exchanging information started using these currencies, as happened in the past with securities, Thus, these digital currencies have become very valuable, and it suffices to know that at the time of writing this article 1 BTC (which is a bitcoin abbreviation) is equal to 9300 USD. The value of this coin in mid-2017 reached more than $ 20,000, Because the process of transferring information on the Internet is done using computers and requires certain capabilities, you can profit from these currencies by mining (using your computer at home and I do not recommend it because it is now impossible to mining at home, you can trade in these same currencies, buy them and they are cheap And sell it when it increases in price, such as trading in shares that we explained earlier.

Characteristics of the cryptocurrency domain:

•Profit by mining is difficult and requires very long time and expensive hardware specifications

•Trading in digital currencies This method is very profitable, and currently there are many companies, services and even banks that deal in these currencies, and there are many who predict that digital currencies will replace ordinary currencies in the near future as well as analytical studies of the arrival of one bitcoin to one million dollars.

Now you have sufficient information in principle

To support you in choosing one or more fields, and I will show you step by step the details of each field .. Are you ready for the million dollar trip?

CHAPTER 1

Digital Marketing

Affiliate Marketing: Affiliate marketing is a real treasure for every young man seeking to change his life for the better in 2020, it opens up great prospects for marketing products and services that are already in the market, and has demand and fame among customers, and then profits through it. Profit opportunities here are limitless.

What is commission or affiliate marketing?

Affiliate Marketing: A marketing system based on the exchange of benefits between the owner of the good, service or offer on the one hand (we will refer to it here in the advertiser), and the publisher or marketer with commission on the other hand.

In commission marketing, the marketer (you) provides marketing services to the advertiser in exchange for a specific commission that is paid according to the agreement, The idea of commission commissioning begins with the advertiser who opens a commission marketing system for the goods, services or offers that he owns. The advertiser, for his part, defines the most important criteria, foundations, and fundamentals that govern his commission marketing system, The commissioner submits a commission to submit an application to participate in this system in accordance with the stated conditions. The publisher is accepted or rejected according to the extent of his compatibility with the criteria and conditions announced by the advertiser, In the event that the publisher accepts work between the advertiser and the publisher, the advertiser pays the publisher through one of the payment methods on the Internet, on top of these methods are bank transfers, electronic banks, the most important of which is **PayPal**.

The idea of commission marketing and why was it found?

In fact, the idea of affiliate is not a product of the existence of the Internet, but it is much older than the existence of the Internet, and it is simply based on mutual benefit as mentioned earlier, Every product or dealer, whatever type of production it produces, markets its products to get the best level of sales, and whatever the marketing power of the product or dealer, it is ultimately limited, so the producers began a long time ago to seek the help of others in marketing their products in exchange for a specific commission, Here, the merchant or owner of the product will get more sales and make more profit, and the marketer will get great commissions according to his marketing efforts, With the emergence of the Internet and the expansion of the idea of marketing through the Internet, the idea of marketing commission or affiliate has become clearer in its clearest, most comprehensive, diversified, widespread and prosperous forms as well. In the past few years, the idea of affiliate has covered many aspects of business and marketing through the Internet.

On the one hand, many companies specializing in commission marketing have emerged, which mainly rely on this type of marketing, On the other hand, the awareness of every business owner has increased online, so he has turned to this type of marketing ... either primarily or as a side.

Some important points about introducing the field of affiliate

1- Commission marketing is not limited to marketing a product or service, but it exceeds that to include every action that is performed by the visitor, starting from subscribing to a mailing list ending with the completion of a complete sale process, including all of their marketing purposes, such as downloading an application or game, Or subscribe to a site, or download a file, etc.

2- The world of commission marketing is a large and varied world, and many specialized sub-types fall under it. Therefore, CPA companies and CPI and CPL companies all fall under the commission marketing system.

3- Every contract or agreement between the advertiser of the owner of a product, service, or commodity with a publisher, and this agreement includes the performance of certain marketing services in exchange for a commission that is commission marketing, even if it is done in a personal manner without the existence of a general system by the advertiser.

4- Sometimes there is a third party in the affiliate system, such as the CPA intermediary companies between the advertiser and the publisher, and at other times there is no third party and the agreement is direct between the advertiser and the publisher, and in the latter case this is achieved either by having an affiliate system in the declared company or by making a special commission marketing contract.

5- Affiliate commission is a variable, not fixed, component. Sometimes the commission is a certain percentage of the price of a good or service, and at other times, it is a pre-determined amount that is paid when the visitor performs a specific action, and this is determined according to the commission marketing system for each advertiser separately or based on The agreement between the advertiser and the publisher.

What do I need to start marketing with commission?

Good product, service, or offer:

On this point I recommend that you choose something you care about and who is personally convinced, as this will facilitate your path in many ways. You can get this either through intermediary companies such as CPA companies, or through the site of the owner of the good or service and subscribe to the affiliate system that it provides, Also if you find the product that you want to market with commission, and when you enter the site you do not find an affiliate system available on the site, in this case you can communicate directly with this site and negotiate with it and reach an appropriate agreement, Since there are a lot of big websites and e-stores available, I will leave the site links and a snapshot of each site at the end of the explanation.

A good source for visitors:

You must have a suitable source of targeted visitors for what you are marketing in order to get a good conversion rate, and then achieve a good level of profits, factors such as the visitor price, level of targeting, amount of visitors and their nature play a key role in this point, But in any case the source of visitors is a very effective component of the commission marketing process, and it has a very big impact on your success as a commission marketer.

Here is a list of the most important visitor sources:

Social Media:

Either free of charge through a page or group interested in what products are marketed, or in a paid format through paid advertising campaigns, Facebook, Instagram, Twitter and LinkedIn, if you have a lot of friends, take advantage of the opportunity and also create commercial pages. People now spend the most part of their time spending on social media, and you are sure of them so be productive and not a consumer.

search engines:

To get visitors from the search engines, there are two ways as well: the first way is through owning a website and making search engine optimization to get free visitors,The second method is by making paid advertising campaigns.

The most important services and tools that each commissioner needs:

I will talk about each tool in general, and how it will benefit you, as I will mention a specific example of each tool, Here I want to mention, that you do not necessarily have to subscribe to the site that we will choose as an example for each tool specifically, and you also do not have to own all the tools we will offer, in some cases you may not need specific tools according to your specific working conditions.

Here are the most important tools and services used in commission marketing:

Good hosting:

In most cases, your success as a commissioner depends on your design of landing pages, especially for what you are marketing, and the landing page for those who do not know is a page that you design to serve as a motivational aspect for the user before entering the advertiser's page, and it helps to increase the conversion rate, and by using it Intelligently, you can completely change the flow of results, One of the good and professional hosting services for my affiliate hosting that I recommend to you: beyondhosting

Tool for making landing pages:

We have previously mentioned the importance of the landing page in your success as a commission marketer, now how can you design a good landing page? In fact, there are many ways to make a landing page, and here we are specifically talking about the tools by which you can make a landing page in an easy and simple way.

Landing page creation tools, are tools that you can, without having experience in the code, create a landing page with good standards, and leadpages are one of the tools you can rely on for this, It is worth noting here that there are alternative ways to make a landing page instead of using one of the tools designated for that, and an alternative ways to work Landing Page hiring specialists (web page designers and developers).

A tool for tracking and analyzing the

results of advertising campaigns:

Almost no real success in working in the field of commission marketing without a good tool for analyzing and following up on advertising campaigns. This is a point full of details and ideas, perhaps I will devote it to a special topic in the future, But to clarify the idea in a simple way, the monitoring and analysis tool is a tool through which you can get a lot of details and information about the performance of your advertising campaigns, You can get very accurate details about your landing page visitors, through these details you can make the necessary adjustments and changes to improve the results of your advertising campaign.

Here is an example for ease of understanding:

Suppose you are marketing the iPhone 8 product with an online store that supports Affiliate system and you are relying on PPV visitors (pay-per-view).

Through the monitoring and analysis tool, you can find

out which keywords or the targeted sites are through which you obtained sales, and which ones you did not obtain sales, and then cancel the lost targets and make a Scale up or upgrade for profitable targets, In fact, the topic is not only limited to that, but the monitoring and analysis tool can give you more like doing a test for a different group of products, and landing pages to see which of them is the best, through only one campaign (this is called split test), In short, the monitoring and analysis tool is the real key to success in commission marketing, and below is one of these good tools that you can rely on as a commission marketer.

https://voluum.com .

Tool to see competitors 'campaigns:

This tool enables you to view some data about advertising campaigns of other commission marketers, With this tool, you can see the landing pages used by other marketers, the source of visitors, and some other targeting data.

You do not have to use this tool to copy other people's campaigns and apply them as they are because it will not work most of the time, but you can use this tool to get more ideas that you can develop, integrate, or apply in other areas of your business, Your choice of this tool depends on the type of visitors you use. For each type of visitor, there are special tools.

Finally, here is an example of one of our great competitors 'campaign reading tools

https://adplexity.com .

Blog owners can also profit from commission marketing:

If you have a blog and get good traffic through search engines, social media, or YouTube, you can also work as a commission marketer, All you have to do here is to find products, services, or offers related to your blog content, and start commission commissioning.

Important tips for your success as a commission marketer:

* The key to your success in the affiliate world is testing and experimenting.

* Do not rely entirely on your successful campaigns at any one time.

* Think outside the box to get exceptional results.

* Get the most revenue in the fastest time from your successful campaigns.

Top Affiliate Marketing Websites:

1. ShareASale Affiliates: ShareASale has been in business 17 years now, and they've definitely kept up with the times. Featuring a plentiful marketplace full of merchants catering to almost everything you can think of, there's always going to be relevant products for you to promote.

2. Solvid Affiliate: We offer a 20% commission on all purchases, including those that are made by the referred client in the future. This means that if you refer a client that spends £3,500/month with Solvid, you will be receiving £700/month for as long as the client stays with us. Similarly, if you refer a client that makes a one-off order of £12,000, you will receive a one-time commission payout of £2,400. Basically, there are no limits to what you can earn. We're simply the highest paying affiliate program in the field! Simply register to access your affiliate account – it's that simple!

3. Amazon Associates: Everyone knows Amazon. The online marketplace that can deliver anything from candy to a fully-functional drone to your door in a day. Every niche has its space on Amazon, which is why it's such a great starting point for an Affiliate Marketing venture.

4. eBay Partners: Even the user-based colossal marketplace that is eBay wants you to help advertise and sell the items on their platform. All you need to do is find listings you want to help promote, promote them using Ebay's Partner Network tools, and you get paid!

5. Shopify Affiliate Program: Shopify is one of the leading eCommerce software used by bloggers and online retailers. As a blogger yourself, you're likely familiar with it. So, for those of you in niches where your audience will also be trying to sell online, Shopify is a great affiliate partnership for you to point them to.

Conclusion: Commission marketing is huge and expanding business, and billions of dollars are traded online every year. As a beginner, you must understand the idea well and prepare your plan (which includes determining the type of visitors and the type of offers or goods that you will market and participate in tools that you think are appropriate for you and are important to your success), then put your focus in one direction and begin testing and experimenting. Keep experimenting until you have reached a successful campaign that will compensate you for all the losses you may lose in the beginning.

CHAPTER 2

Content Industry

YouTube partner: Creating a YouTube channel represents a dream for many, as YouTube is an opportunity for everyone to be creative and creative, and to share the world with passion, talents and interests, in addition to the huge profitable opportunities that can be achieved through it, Whether your goal in creating a YouTube channel is to make money from YouTube, or to share others with your passion and interests, or to serve a specific intellectual or community issue, or even to market your business, of course you want to create a successful and professional YouTube channel.

In this book, I will explain the steps to create a YouTube channel in an easy and simple way

I will address the most important settings that will make your channel look professional to your audience.

Why is profit from YouTube

an exceptional opportunity for everyone?

* Video in general and YouTube in particular is an excellent way to communicate any idea in an easy, simple and effective way for Internet users.

* The internet user is often lazy, so he prefers to see what he wants on the Internet with less means to exert effort, and this is precisely what YouTube videos provide.

* According to the statistics about YouTube, it alone attracts nearly two billion users per month.

* Because of the profit sharing system provided by YouTube, video producers have become more motivating to make videos in a highly efficient and professional way and to cover all human interests.

* Based on this, YouTube users have come to trust it as a search engine and use it not only for entertainment, but they use it to answer all their questions and solve all their problems.

* YouTube represents an opportunity for every person who has a passion or interest, to turn this passion or interest into an opportunity to make a profitable and growing profit.

* YouTube is not an opportunity for a certain class of content creators, but it opens up new opportunities and opportunities for photographers, video designers, actors, directors, etc.

* In short, YouTube is an online version of the world of cinema and television, but it is a more innovative and flexible version, and its doors are open to everyone without distinction, and you have every right to enter through its open doors.

What do I need to start earning from YouTube?

YouTube Channel Idea:

This point is considered the most important and most dangerous point ever on the way to profit from YouTube, and if implemented smartly and wisely, it cuts a lot of effort and wasted time in the future, In order to test the possibility of a successful YouTube channel idea, you must evaluate it according to two main axes:

They will be expressed here through these

two questions:

The first question: Will your channel be around an idea you really are good at?

There is always a common factor among all YouTube stars, or let's say between all successful and popular YouTube channels, this factor is that they are really good at what they do, Let's take, for example, one of the famous and successful YouTube channels specialized in teaching make-up to girls. You will find that the girl with the channel or introduction to the article is really interested in the world of makeup, She has great knowledge about this world, and she will always find her seeking knowledge and learning about the makeup field to offer something new to her followers, Here, as a person looking to profit from YouTube, you should have the idea of a YouTube channel that revolves around a field that you really are interested in, knowledgeable and knowledgeable about it, and you have a passion and love to always learn in this field.

The second question: Is there an audience that is interested in what you intend to present on your

channel?

Suppose in the previous point that you are interested in astronomy and space and intend to create a YouTube channel on this topic, in the following point you must measure the size of your expected audience:

Here are some points that will help you understand the size of your potential audience:

* Use the Google Tool to measure the keyword search rate (Keyword Planner), enter the most important keywords around which your channel will revolve, and record the monthly search rates for each word.

* Search YouTube for channels similar to the one you would like to create, and note the number of subscriptions in each (remember that the small number of subscribers may be due to the poor quality of the channels, and not to the lack of an interested audience).

* Also, you should search for videos similar to what you would like to present on your channel. Some channels that offer various content may contain one or more videos related to your channel idea, also without the number of views for each video.

* Search the social media for groups or pages that talk about ideas that are identical or similar to your channel idea, and without the size of these groups and the level of interaction with them.

A set of skills:

Now you have an idea for a YouTube channel according to your interests and passions, which you found to have a large segment of the audience already interested ... very cool now you have to know what skills you need to start implementing the idea.

Although working as a YouTube publisher is something flexible, and you can start with the lowest possible capabilities, there are some important skills that you have in case you want to create a promising YouTube channel with a fast growth rate, I will list you with the most important skills required in the YouTube world, but this does not necessarily mean that you need all of them to start your channel and profit from it, as there are certain skills that you will not need depending on the nature of your channel, Also it is important to say that most successful and profitable YouTube channels are not based on one person, but behind an entire team working together with different disciplines, so you as a channel owner do not have all the skills we will mention below:

The first skill: speaking, delivering, acting, explaining and commenting:

Of course, you have the skill that is appropriate to the nature of the content that you intend to present on your channel, and for clarification, let's continue with our example of space and astronomy ... You have to have good skills in communicating information and commenting on hot news in the space world, and the ability to explain and simplify difficult concepts..etc.

The second skill: photography:

Video quality is a very important component of getting more views, and then making more profits. Of course, video quality depends largely on the photography skills of the photographer.

The third skill: montage, editing and directing:

Good photography without good output is nothing, so in order to complete the good filming of videos, there must also be skills to produce this photography professionally, and this requires some effort in learning and gaining experience.

Fourth skill: Marketing:

Everything that happens through the Internet requires marketing efforts in order to bear fruit, and this applies to profit from YouTube as well, As a YouTube channel owner, you have to have some knowledge and skill on how to market your videos and channel, whether through YouTube itself or through other social media, or through a separate blog for your YouTube channel.

What do you do if you do not have the skill you need to earn from YouTube?

What if you do not have some of the skills listed above and want to start under any circumstances, is there a good alternative that you can rely on without having to learn all these skills? In fact, yes, there is an alternative.

The alternative here is to use external sources to complete specific tasks that you do not know. For example, you can rely on yourself in the filming stage (if you are good at that), and rely on external sources in the editing phase, for example, there are many websites that are alternative to the complex montage programs that you can rely on Free or larger and more professional capabilities with small amounts, and also online design sites to design photos or buy designs at cheap prices on free work platforms according to your request, but you can start completely free of charge. I will leave you sites to help you implement the montage for free:

* filmora wondershare (100$) software

* promo (29$ or 59$ or 209$) online

* flexclip (free or 5$ or 8$) online

* movie maker (Free) software

Steps to profit from YouTube

create a YouTube channel:

Creating a YouTube channel is a very easy matter, and it requires no more than one Google account, and with some simple steps you can choose a suitable name for your channel, and then start preparing it in terms of description, its own image..etc.

Start to supply your channel with videos consistently and continuously:

Start with all your strength, and try to implement catchy and interesting video ideas at first, with which you can attract subscribers to your channel, Keep publishing new videos, and try to avoid the mistakes that you made in previous videos, listen to your audience even if it was a little in the beginning, try to please it and benefit from its advice and suggestions, and encourage it to share its opinions always.

Start marketing your channel and videos:

* Create pages on the social media of your YouTube channel.

* Create paid advertising campaigns on YouTube.

* Ask your friends, family and loved ones for help to help your videos reach more viewers.

* Try to reach mutual marketing agreements with channel owners in the same field or near fields.

* Try to use the trend to get more views (using the trend means making videos about hot events or popular videos).

* Encourage viewers of your videos to subscribe to the channel, and share the videos on social media.

* Create a blog for your YouTube channel, and post textual content about her videos.

start making money from YouTube:

There are a lot of ways to profit from YouTube as mentioned above, but the most important and best known is through participation in the YouTube Partner Program, It is worth noting that there are conditions for joining the YouTube Partner Program, which must be met in order to activate the profit from the channel, which YouTube calls: "eligibility requirements to join the program."

Here is a list of YouTube terms or requirements for profit:

* The channel is in compliance with YouTube monet-

ization policies.

* Be resident in a country where the YouTube Partner Program is available.

* 4000 watch hours in the last 12 months.

At least 1000 subscribers.

* Having a Google AdSense account and linking it to the channel.

* The profit rate from YouTube

One of the important questions that concern many of those looking to profit from YouTube, is **"How much profit from YouTube?"**.

The profit rate from YouTube ranges from $ 100 to more than a million dollars a month.

And the rate of profit from YouTube depends on many variables, the most important of which are:

The first "changer": the geographical distribution of viewers Of course, the American viewer makes more profit than the Egyptian viewer.

The second "variable": the channel specialty YouTube works with a targeted system to show the right ads in front of the right viewer, and of course the nature of the content of your YouTube channel attracts viewers who have certain interests.

For example, if your channel is reviewing the types of smartphones, it will naturally attract those interested in buying new smartphones, and then they will have ads for electronic stores selling smartphones in front of them, If your channel was about the space world, it would attract another type of viewer, and then another kind of advertisement, Of course the price of a click or watch on each ad differs from one another, so the rate of profit is affected by the quality of the ads that are affected by the nature of the content of your YouTube channel.

The last variable" video length" A 3-minute video earns less profit than a 15-minute video, because more than one ad can be placed in it, but you have to consider how long the viewer will be watching the video,The viewer may have left the 15-minute video after the second minute in a situation that was not attractive enough.

CHAPTER 3

websites

Every professional way to earn money online should start with creating a website. So we can say that there are many, many ways to profit from websites.

In this book I will present to you a list of the most important and famous ways to profit from websites.

The most important ways to profit from websites

Profit from websites through Google AdSense:

Google AdSense is the most popular way to profit from websites that specialize in providing content for visitors (i.e. blogs), and in fact working as a publisher with Google AdSense has many advantages, One of these advantages is the ease of implementation, in the case of your work as a publisher with Google AdSense, all that is required of you is to have an account with them, then you create ad units and place them on your site through a simple code.

For those who have no idea what Google AdSense is, it is a company specialized in advertising and it works as a mediator between advertisers who want to get visitors to their sites, or for their landing pages, and publishers i.e. website owners who want to get income from their websites, Google AdSense has special policies and standards for accepting its publishers, and on top of these criteria, the site does not have any illegal content, and that the site contains content of a high level of quality and efficiency and provides benefit to the visitor.

Profit from websites through Google AdSense alternatives:

Of course, Google AdSense is the most famous and most important company in the profit from the websites that offer content, but it is not the only company specialized in that, There are a lot of other companies that you can subscribe to place ads on your site and get profits from them, among the most famous of these AdSense competitors, which are managed through the search engines Ping and Yahoo are the media company.

Profit from websites through Native ads companies: Native ads is a term that has recently appeared in the world of e-marketing, which means local ads or self-ads, Native ads represent a new generation of ads, These ads appear on the websites as if they were affiliated with the site and not advertisements of external websites or products, These ads appear just below the article, under other articles of your choice, or related topics. And in it a list of articles is developed for other advertisers' sites, and it is along with articles from the same site, Recently, Google AdSense made this kind of ads available to publishers, but there are companies that specialize in Native ads that you can subscribe to in order to make profits from your website, and one of the most famous of these companies: Taboola & Outbrain.

Profit from websites through affiliate or commission marketing: This is a more advanced option compared to Google AdSense, and better profits can be made through it if it is managed properly. In fact, this method is not suitable for every site, but it is a great option for each site that specializes in one subject deeply.

For example, if you have a website that talks about car insurance, you provide articles and advice about the best insurance companies, and the optimal system for each case ... etc. Here, commission marketing is the best option for you, Of course, with the increase in the number of products and services on the Internet, and with the owners of these products and those services resorting to the idea of commission marketing, the idea of commission marketing has become possible for many sites in many specialties, I have already explained at the top in e-marketing about affiliate, and this is a form that can be applied.

Profit from the websites by renting advertising space: If you have a site with attractive topics, and your site gets a good number of visitors. It is possible that you get special offers to buy advertising space on your site, you can make good profits from your site if you can reach the right advertiser, All you have to do in the beginning is to take advantage of the advertising space on your site to announce the presence of vacant advertising space, and then the offers will follow.

Profit from websites by selling products or services: If you have a concrete product or a digital product, you can sell it through your website and make profits through it, Also if you have a service that you can provide to others in return for money, then you can also use your website to sell it and make profits through it.

I will explain in detail later on electronic stores in a separate topic.

Profit from websites by creating and selling them: One of the great and innovative ways to make profits from websites is by creating the site and investing some effort, time and money until it starts to get a good level of profits, and in the end, selling it with a good profit margin, The cool thing about it is that this process can be repeated to build sites continuously for sale at the end, You can sell your site through the most popular sites that specialize in **Flippa** site trading.

CHAPTER 4

E-Commerce

Online Store: It is an electronic platform (website) through which tangible or intangible products are sold through the internet. Also, the online store can specialize in selling services.

Steps to create a professional online store:

Step 1: Deciding which product to sell in your online store

There are mostly two situations behind creating an online store: The first case: is to expand the scope and sales of a store that is already on the ground, by taking advantage of the opportunities and profit potential offered by e-commerce.

The second case: creating an online store as a new and independent project, and this is what we will talk about here, In order to start your online store as a new and independent venture, you need to decide which product or products to sell.

Here you have one of two directions:

The first direction: the unique and innovative product,

which requires a new idea based on the needs of the target audience, and which can be an innovative tool, for example, to facilitate life or solve a problem. This trend needs an innovative and creative person, and the risk is very high, but the profitability opportunities are also very high.

The second direction: the traditional product known to everyone, and this includes all kinds of products found in the market, such as clothes, electrical appliances, cosmetics, etc. This is the type on which we will complete our topic.

Here are some points that will help you determine the product for your online store:

* Brainstorming sessions, in which you can get more product ideas through your own needs.

* Opinion poll of friends and relatives.

* Benefiting from the experiences of others, by following other e-stores and knowing the products that you sell.

* Conducting research on the internet about the most important products consumed in the target market.

Step two: check the ability to sell this product:

After you've determined your product idea, let's say here you decide to create an online clothing store.

You have to put this idea to the test and check to verify its usefulness, and you have to make sure that you are able to sell the product you selected, this requires you to conduct market research, and understand the rates of demand for this product.

A tool like the Google Keyword Tool will help you a lot in understanding demand rates based on knowing the search rates in the Google search engine on a specific good.

Suppose here that you are considering creating an online clothing store, but you have not yet decided whether you will sell clothes in general, or will specialize in children's clothing.

Type the word children's clothing on Google, to understand the monthly search rate on it, of course the higher the search rate the higher the demand for the product is also high.

But we must point out here a very important point: that the high rate of demand also means a high level of competition (that is, there are electronic stores already selling the same product because it has a large demand).

Of course, the decision is up to you according to the competitive advantages you possess, and a well thought out marketing plan for your online store.

In this step, you also have to search the Internet for competing stores (specializing in children's clothing) that target the same market you intend to target. You have to check the strengths and weaknesses of the competing stores, and of course it is best to make a purchase through them, in order to verify everything based on real experience.

This will give you an idea of your level of competitiveness, and hence the ability to sell the product.

The third step: Determine the source of obtaining the product that you will sell:

Suppose in the previous step, you decided that children's clothing are the products that you will sell in your online store. In this step you have to determine the source from which you will get these children's clothes.

In this step there are three options that you can choose between:

Produce the product in your own factory:

This is the most difficult and risky option, in addition to that it needs more time and effort, and then this option is the least likely for the majority.

Using Drop Shipping:

Drop shipping: It is a type of business, in which you, as a store owner, market the products, put them in your own store, set their price, and sell them to the consumer under your store name, but the products are to a third party (big store or wholesaler).

Once the buyer has purchased the product, it is ordered from the primary store and delivered to the buyer. Here the process of storing and delivering is entirely through the main store, and your online store is just an intermediary. It is worth noting that the shipping way is the easiest and least risky option

Buy from wholesalers or factories:

This is the standard or traditional option, and it is the most popular option in the world of electronic stores, in which you, as the owner of an electronic store, buy the product from one of the wholesalers or directly from the factory and store it in your own warehouse to prepare for purchase requests through your online store.

Step 4: Determine how to create an online e-store

There are three ways to create an online store, and this is an explanation for you: Create an online store by a specialized programming company, or through a professional programmer.

This method is the most difficult and the most expensive, and in it the programmer writes the e-store code from A to Z, so every time you want to make an adjustment to anything, you should refer to the programmer.

This method requires a professional programmer and a specialist in electronic store programming, it is suitable for large stores, where unique design and exceptional features and features can be made for the electronic store, but it is not suitable for emerging stores due to the high cost and difficulty in obtaining a professional programmer.

In this way to create an online store you need a good website hosting and domain name, in addition to the programmer.

Create an online store via WordPress:

To create an online store using WordPress, follow these steps:

* Book a good web hosting that supports WordPress.

* Purchase a domain name for your online store.

* Choose a custom WordPress e-commerce template.

* Setting a WordPress e-commerce plugin (WooCommerce).

Create an e-store through specialized e-commerce platforms:

There are integrated services for creating electronic stores, these services give you everything you need to build a professional electronic store, and this is what these platforms give you:

* With it you can buy the domain name and link it to the platform in a few minutes.

* It gives you an easy control panel to create your store, which even non-professionals can handle it easily.

*Provides your e-shop with ready-made templates, it gives you a set of templates for free, and gives you more other templates while you want to buy.

*A control panel allows you to adjust your store design, so that your store is unique in shape and color.

* Provide you with a support service.

* With it, you can easily set the payment method, which itself provides some payment services.

* This option to create a professional online store is the easiest ever, and does not require any specialist skills, but it is the most expensive.

* There are a lot of e-store creation platforms and here are the most famous: Shopify & Bigcommerce & wix & etsy .

Step 5: Defining the payment method in your online store (payment gateway):

This is a very important and vital step for your online store, and it depends heavily on your choice in the step that preceded it. For example, there are some platforms that allow payment gateway service such as Shopify platform.

First, let's clarify what is meant by the term (payment gateway).

payment gateways are companies that specialize in providing payment solutions on the Internet. These services manage the payment in your online store completely for a commission.

By creating an account with it and linking it to your store, these companies receive money from buyers, and transfer it into your account with them, through which you can receive your money on your bank account.

There are many, many payment gateways and here are the most important:

PayPal:

Obviously, it is one of the oldest and most popular payment solutions on the Internet, it is basically an electronic bank for everyone, but it provides a payment gateway for every electronic store owner by creating a business account.

General advice on creating a professional online store:

* Always be flexible and think outside the box.
* Pay attention to the legal crack and avoid inadvertently breaking the law.
* Because we are talking about an online store, there must be a good plan for doing e-marketing.
* I want to remind you that the initiation of ideas is the most important step at all.

Yes, you will face obstacles but every obstacle can be overcome as long as you take the first step.

CHAPTER 5

Facebook Marketplace

There is no doubt that everyone who reads this article uses the social networking site Facebook, and the majority of those who use Facebook use it for entertainment and communication with friends, but what many Facebook users do not know is the wonderful marketing and profitability features that Facebook offers, including the Facebook Marketplace.

In this book I will talk about Facebook Marketplace in many aspects, so that you can use this feature in the best possible way.

What is the Facebook Marketplace?

Facebook Marketplace: It is a Facebook place where you can offer your products for sale, or view products not offered for sale for purchase. Facebook Market Place is a service recently provided by Facebook, this service enables Facebook users to buy and sell through Facebook.

Products are displayed on the Facebook Marketplace according to geographical classification, meaning that the seller who lives in Florida shows his products to users who live in Florida as well.

Facebook Marketplace service first appeared in October 2016 as a simulation of Craigslist for classified ads of used products, the service was available in a small group of countries (only 4 countries), but over time it became available in almost every country in the world, in addition to Facebook's work to expand The scope of this service includes many aspects and includes many advantages.

Some important points for the Facebook Marketplace:

* Facebook Marketplace is a place dedicated to selling used and new products among members of the Facebook community. It is an attempt by Facebook to keep pace with the explosive growth of e-commerce by facilitating the idea of buying and selling among Facebook users.

* Facebook Marketplace is a completely free service for all Facebook users. Facebook does not charge any commission for offering products for sale, or any other type of commission.

* Facebook Marketplace is a place where only the seller and the buyer meet, but it does not include the mediation of payments, or the delivery of the product from the seller to the buyer.

* As an arrangement on the previous point, Facebook is not directly responsible for scams that may occur through the Facebook Marketplace, but it provides a system for evaluating sellers and buyers to help users avoid fraud, and it also allows the feature of reporting infringing products and forged or fraudulent accounts.

* Facebook Marketplace is a place to display all kinds of tangible products, from clothes to real estate, through cars, electronic devices, etc. These products are categorized into 9 main divisions, each with sub-divisions.

* Buying and selling groups are part of the Facebook Marketplace, and results can be filtered in the Marketplace so that they only come from groups that the user is a member of.

* Facebook Marketplace is not only a place to sell products, but services can also be sold (but this is only available in some countries).

Conclusion: Facebook Marketplace is a genius solution for everyone who wants to achieve sales through the Internet, completely free of charge. In just a few minutes, you can add your products through your personal Facebook account, and start achieving sales.

Recently Facebook started to open the door for store and store owners to put their products or services on its Marketplace, this service is still only available in the United States.

Achieving sales through Facebook Market Place is an extremely easy task, thanks to the targeting system that is based on the artificial intelligence used by Facebook, you just have to add your product while following the advice that was mentioned, and within hours you will receive messages from potential buyers who want to buy your product, And it is completely free.

CHAPTER 6

Digital currencies

Bitcoin has become the talk of the hour in the past few months. In fact, it is the talk of the hour on the economic and technological level since it was established and became famous.

How not to be the talk of the hour, and it is considered an amazing invention that has a great resonance in the global economy.

In recent months, the bitcoin currency has gained exceptional popularity, after the rise in the price of one bitcoin to nearly twenty thousand dollars.

Bitcoin witnessed a sudden catastrophic decline, bringing the price of bitcoin to nearly six thousand dollars.

Since then the price curve has started to rise again, now reaching almost $ 10,000

After the Corona crisis and the coming economic crises, bitcoin is expected to increase suddenly to reach one million dollars.

What is Bitcoin?

(Bitcoin) is one of the Cryptocurrency that has no

physical balance on the ground. It is well known that money issued by countries has a golden balance.

As for Bitcoin here, it is a completely independent currency that does not have any gold balance, and has no physical presence on the ground in any way.

Bitcoin is a decentralized currency that is not subject to any centralized system or specific country.

This means that bitcoin is a standalone, peer-to-peer financial system without any intermediation between traders.

In the financial system accepted in all countries of the world, the circulation of money on the largest level is through banks, according to the policies of countries.

In Bitcoin, there is no middleman, as you can transfer any amount of money from your wallet to anyone else directly and almost without commission.

Bitcoin is a cryptocurrency or encrypted meaning that the personal data of any owner of this currency is not disclosed.

How did Bitcoin originate and in what year?

Satoshi Nakamoto is the name behind Bitcoin's coinage. It is an unknown name and the identity of this name has not been known yet.

Perhaps it is a real person's name or a pseudonym for a person or group of people, or even a pseudonym for a project launched by a company or country.

Bitcoin was released as an open program in 2009. What is meant here with an open source program is that anyone can take a copy of this program, make adjustments to it, and create a new digital currency.

Is bitcoin unique?

Bitcoin is the first digital currency of its kind, but it is not the only one. After the emergence of Bitcoin, many other digital currencies appeared.

Among the most famous and most important:

* Ethereum * Ripple * Litecoin

 * Dogecoin * Dash * Zcash

What are the ways to get bitcoin?

There are two ways to obtain Bitcoin:

Mining: It is a system that is built by high-speed computers with special specifications. In order to solve some complex mathematical equations and problems. When these parameters are resolved, the system gives you Bitcoin units and you can add them to your account or personal wallet.

Through people with Bitcoin credit:

You can get Bitcoin credit by purchasing it from one of the people or brokers working in this field. Or, you can get it by selling products or providing services to others, and making Bitcoin the payment method.

Is there an unlimited Bitcoin mining?

Satoshi Nakamoto didn't randomly set up a Bitcoin system, but set up a hermetic system for everything. Having an infinite number of Bitcoin is not a smart choice for someone who has created such a genius system. There are only 21 million bitcoins that can be mined. After completing their mining, no new quantities will be released for mining. It is worth noting that 80% of the total bitcoin amount (21 million bitcoin) has been mined to date. But the remaining small amount (which represents 20%) will be mined for more than 120 years. *It is estimated that the last bitcoin will be mining by 2145.*

What is the process of Bitcoin mining?

This is the toughest question in Bitcoin. The mining process is a complex process and has many aspects, so it is the most difficult to understand process for many. Here I will try to simplify the answer without going into the mining process from the technical complex.

Also, traditional currencies need banks and governments in order to be organized and managed and to ensure the correctness of trading operations through them. So Bitcoin also needs someone to do this job.

We have mentioned above that Bitcoin is a decentralized currency, that is, there is no specific entity to manage and regulate dealings with:

* Hence the importance of the mining process. The mining process includes the following:

* Activate transfers between and some accounts and verify them This is to ensure the Bitcoin security system.

* The aggregation of the last set of trading or transfer operations (a few hundred transactions) and placing them in what is called a block or transactions block.

* The bitcoin system requires solving a set of complex mathematical equations in order for each new block to be approved and included in the block chain.

* When one of the miners arrives to solve the required mathematical equations, the mass of the new coefficients is included in the block chain.

* In contrast, the bitcoin system is designed to give 12.5 bitcoins to the metal that came to solve equations first.

* Every 10 minutes, a set of transactions representing a new block of transactions is released.

* Every approximately 4 years, the Bitcoin number granted to regulate each block of transactions is halved.

* The prize for adding a new block was 50 bitcoins in 2009.

*Then it decreased to 25 Bitcoin four years later, and now the prize for adding a new block has become only 12.5 Bitcoin.

*Also, the number of bitcoins mined in a new form decreases every 4 years.

*In the first stage that started in 2009 (the year the Bitcoin system was created) 10 and a half million new Bitcoins were mined, which is half of the total amount of Bitcoin (12 million).

*In the next four years, half of the remaining 5.25 million bitcoins were mined. By this amount, half of it is mined in the next stage (each stage consists of approximately four years). Thus the system continues so that the last mining stage is just one bitcoin fraction.

"This explains that the last bitcoin will be almost mined in the year 2145".

What does blockchain mean?

Blockchain means, which is a comprehensive history of all Bitcoin transactions since its inception. A block chain consists of blocks, or as I mentioned above, a new block is added to the block chain every 10 minutes. The bottom line is that the blockchain represents an account book for every transaction made since Bitcoin was created.

What is the secret of Bitcoin security?

The bitcoin system is considered one of the strongest secure electronic systems (it is very difficult to penetrate if not impossible) The secret of this security is based on the encryption system that Bitcoin enjoys on the one hand, and on the other hand because all transactions are recorded on hundreds of thousands of devices (mining devices). Which is almost impossible to penetrate all of them to make an illegal transfer, for example.

From this we conclude that the mining process is the secret behind Bitcoin's survival, If all the miners abandoned their role, the system would collapse (and this explains the motivational grants for the two minerals (12.5 Bitcoin reward for those who come to solve the equations of one block).

What do I need to get started in the mining process?

First, let's make sure that the mining process gets more difficult over time, When the Bitcoin system first appeared, miners could do the mining.

As for now, the mining process needs high-speed computers with special specifications, it works through mining programs, do not try to mining at home, but to invest in bitcoin you have to buy bitcoin or some of the Satoshi and save it for the future, when the price of it increases immediately, you may become wealthy of One day, the price of bitcoin today is in 2020, $ 10,000, if you own one bitcoin, or half of bitcoin today, and save it in the electronic wallet, it is expected that in the year 2021 the price of one bitcoin will reach $ 1 million $ 10,000,000, suddenly and unprecedentedly, with a rise in its price. Then you will have earned $ 990,000 in less than one year. You can also invest in other digital currencies such as (Stellar) currency, which is now 0.08 cents or an Ethereum, which is now $ 245. After bitcoin becomes one million dollars, all other digital currencies will be affected by the rise so you can imagine how much profits:

The price of the steel is 0.08 cents now in the year 2020, and you bought 500 (Stellar) for 40 dollars, so expect after 4 years (Stellar) rise to the price of 1000 dollars. You now have half a million dollars in only invest $ 40. But do not forget that these expectations can be right and wrong.

What is Bitcoin wallet?

* Bitcoin wallet: is a way for you to join the Bitcoin community.

* The bitcoin wallet function is similar to the wallet function in which you keep your paper money.

* Through the Bitcoin Portfolio you can send and receive bitcoin currency.

*You can transfer Bitcoin to anyone else who has a Bitcoin account. You can also buy from any store that offers bitcoin as a payment method.

There are many types of bitcoin portfolio and these are the most famous and the most important:

Bitcoin wallet on your mobile phone:

In this case, your Bitcoin wallet is an application that you can install on your mobile phone to conduct your transactions in Bitcoin:

Bitcoin wallet on your computer:

It is a program that you can download to your personal computer, very similar to the first type, but the difference here is that it is intended for computers.

Bitcoin wallet concrete:

It is a special and independent device. You can carry in your bag wherever you go and you can conduct your transactions in Bitcoin.

Bitcoin wallet for the web:

It is a service provided by some sites. With it, you can create and manage a Bitcoin wallet over the Internet from any device, from anywhere, The bottom line is that Bitcoin wallet is software that is installed on your mobile device or computer, or on a separate device. Or on one of the sites online, This software gives you control of your bitcoin balance (send and receive bitcoin) through your login information.

How widespread is Bitcoin use?

In fact, the results of the spread of Bitcoin so far are impressive.
Here are some data that show how widespread Bitcoin is used around the world:

* There are many countries in the world that are considered Bitcoin legal or called the friendly countries of Bitcoin.

*These countries include Canada, Australia, Japan, the United States, and England.

* There are a lot of ATM exchange machines with which you can withdraw funds with your bitcoin balance.

*There are many shops, shops and restaurants on the ground that accept bitcoin payments.

* There are many markets for services and products that accept Bitcoin payments online Including : Microsoft, PayPal, newegg, Overstock.

* finally, there is no better evidence for the spread of bitcoin more than, that the price of one bitcoin today is 10,000 dollars.

WARNINGS

Do not spend your savings on your immediate desires.

Do not work with minimum wages. Business owners will not be late to pay you less money as long as it is legal.

Do not forget to take advantage of your savings and invest it, otherwise you will not reap any harvest.

Investment advice: Do not eat all of your seeds and do not eat all the eggs of the chicken you own (to produce any crops and you will not have any new strains of chicken left!)

All your chickens will grow old and will not produce any income for you in the future

Finally, I hope you become a happy millionaire in your life

www.ingramcontent.com/pod-product-compliance
Lightning Source LLC
Chambersburg PA
CBHW030524220526
45463CB00007B/2701